THE ART OF TRAVELING - IN THE FOOTHILLS OF THE SOUTHERN ALPS

Jorn Heldrup
132, Stenlokken
3460 Birkerod
Danmark
Cell: +45 51 23 82 47
heldrupj@dadlnet.dk

"You should rest without interruption and forget your former life. Let your eyes unlearn what they have seen; let your ears grow accustomed to more healthful words. Every time you go out, your old desires are stirred anew, even before you reach your destination"

-Lucius Annaeus Seneca

Introduction

This is not a traditional guidebook but an inspiration and adventure guide for people visiting places off the beaten track.

There are many guidebooks covering the Italian and Swiss lakes in the Southern Alps, and the author recommends that you familiarize yourself with the areas covered by this book and buy the relevant maps before your journey.

Please do not hesitate to contact the author with your comments and suggestions for the book's next edition.

This book is based on numerous trips to the areas in question over the last ten years. In this respect, I would like to thank my traveling companions for their company and feedback on the places mentioned in the book. Tania Charlton Christensen, Anne Charlton Christensen, and Edward Murphy joined me on many trips.

The author took all the photos in the book. Magic Earth and AllTrails provided the maps.

Table of Contents

Chapter One: The Art of Traveling

Traditional boat, El Nido, Nothern Palawan, Phillipines

One can argue that traveling is an art form that can be perfected over time. I have traveled extensively throughout my professional life since my work involved frequent travel to countries worldwide. When I add the places I have visited on my holidays, I have visited around 120 countries and territories. Besides travel, I have lived and worked in five countries.

Even after leaving full-time work, I have enjoyed traveling to places I have not visited before and frequently returning to my favorite countries, including France, Italy, and Switzerland. My family and friends have increasingly wondered why I keep traveling, which made me wonder where this drive for travel was coming from.

Most people I know like to travel but usually go twice or thrice a year. I, however, spend more and more time traveling, and it quickly adds up to three to four months a year, covering up to ten individual trips. After thinking about it for quite some time, I wondered if it could be linked to my DNA.

Over the last couple of years, I studied my ancestry, supported by several DNA tests, to better understand my family roots and origins. Looking at my immediate family, finding a person with the same urge to travel was hard. But then I realized that my grandfather on my mother's side had been working on one of the ocean liners that took emigrants from Sweden to the United States. He had spent many years traveling back and forth between Gothenburg and New York and even on a cruise to the Caribbean in the 1930s.

Roger Fredrik Oscar Nilsson and his older brother Gastor Oskar William Nilsson were the only ancestors I could identify who had this desire to travel and had spent many years of their lives doing it. Today, people might find it unusual that particular individuals crave to travel, but if we go back to our past, we might identify the origins of this tendency.

Nomad comes from the Latin word 'nomas,' which means wandering shepherd. One particular nomadic group, 'The Yamnaya People,' had a unique role in Europe by migrating into Western Europe during the 3rd millennium BC. They lived primarily as nomads in the area covering southern Ukraine and Russia. They had domesticated horses and manufactured ceramics, tools, and weapons. Nomads like the Yamnaya people were widespread in Europe for more than 3,000 years, and it is no wonder that nomadic traits have been hardwired into our DNA. So, I was not surprised when I discovered that I shared DNA with the Yamnaya people.

You don't have to be a nomad to enjoy traveling, but you might benefit from the experiences of frequent travelers. Traveling exposes us to different landscapes, climates, cultures, livelihoods, food, and historical settings. It's also an occasion to engage in physical activities in nature, whether swimming, hiking, cycling, rowing, or sailing.

It is tempting to have your travels prearranged by a travel agency, let them decide where to go, and have them arrange all the excursions and accommodation at a particular destination. Below, you will find some of the lessons I have learned from extensive traveling since the 1970s.

- Plan trips well in advance, as this usually allows you to find cheaper flights and more accommodation options.

- Plan the trip yourself unless you are going to a country with poor infrastructure, significant security challenges, a completely unknown culture or language, or an activity where you need a reliable local guide.

- By planning the travel yourself, you will get to know the country or area you are traveling to beforehand, allowing you to make more informed decisions about your travel plans.

- Find information on the local climatic conditions to time your visit to your needs and expectations.

- It is usually better to focus on a few places and get to know them better rather than rushing around to many locations within a limited period.

- Arrange your travel plans so that you have plenty of opportunities to spend time in nature.

- Renting private accommodation often gives you more exposure to the people in the area and access to recommendations and advice on things to do.

- On longer trips, it might be a good idea to have unplanned periods to allow the impressions and suggestions to guide your travels.

- Maps, especially hiking and bicycle maps, can be challenging to find locally. Therefore, it is wise to acquire them before your departure.

- An increasing number of places have been flooded with tourists during high season. Avoid these places unless you want to meet your neighbors while traveling. Besides, if you aim to meet local people in an area, you won't find them there.

- Before you leave, study the latest travel advice and ensure you have the relevant immunizations and prophylactic medicine, and if relevant, an impregnated bednet and insecticide for malaria.

- Include a small professional first aid kit in your hand luggage, and make sure to have the relevant plugs and adapters for your destination(s).

- Travel light and try only to use carry-on bags when flying.

Chapter Two: What Makes the Foothills of the Southern Alps Special?

Lago di Como, as seen from Lierna on the Eastern shore

You will find some of the most spectacular lakes in Europe in the foothills of the Southern Alps. The lakes support a unique, humid subtropical climate that explains the rich vegetation around the lakes, including wine, olive trees, banana palms, and a wide variety of trees and flowers like Nerium and Hibiscus. The vegetation is very similar to that found on the Mediterranean coast in Italy and France. The summers are, however, more humid at the lakes and give rise to strong but often short thunderstorms during the summer months.

The many lakes in Northern Italy, including the two lakes shared with Switzerland, are supplied with water from the Alps, which can be observed from all the lakes. Glaciers of the sub-alpine region originally formed the lakes.

The lakes are central to people's lives and are still used for transport, sailing, swimming, and all kinds of water sports. They also set the scene for the many small towns and villages around the lakes and the tree-lined promenades full of cafes and restaurants.

Even if you come from the nearby mountains or the Po Valley, you will be surprised how quickly the vegetation, climate, and atmosphere change when you reach the lakes.

When Homo Sapiens arrived in Southern Europe some forty thousand years ago, some of them settled by the lakes. They were hunter-gatherers living in the area before the last ice age. When the climate turned warmer some twenty to ten thousand years ago, people began to settle around the lakes again. Numerous archeological sites in the region illustrate the transformation of the living conditions and the culture up to the Roman period.

Toward the end of the 18th Century and the beginning of the 19th Century, some towns, like Lugano and

Como, became tourist hubs, with numerous hotels and a tourist industry catering to wealthy Europeans.

Today, the lakes are popular tourist destinations throughout the year, and many foreigners have chosen them as their primary or secondary homes. Italians from the Northern Po Valley also have holiday homes or primary homes and can easily commute to work in the towns south of the lakes. The lakes are also popular weekend destinations.

The following chapters include short presentations of most of the area's lakes and suggestions on places to stay and visit.

THE ART OF TRAVELLELING
- IN THE FOOTHILLS OF THE SOUTHERN ALPS

Chapter Three: Verbania

Verbania on Lago Maggiore

What makes Verbania unique?

Verbania is a short ride from Milan but a relaxed place away from the city's madding crowd. The town is located on the western side of Lake Maggiore (Lago Maggiore) and is well-situated for visiting the many attractions. Lake Orta (Lago d'Orta) is located southwest of the town, and Lake Lugano (Lago di Logano) is to the east. Therefore, I suggest using Verbania as your base for visiting the three lakes.

Verbania is a town with a population of just over 30,000 people. The town is divided into two main centers. Intra is the modern section of town where most inhabitants live and where the car ferry servicing Laveno on the eastern side of the lake originates. With Roman origins, Pallanza, the historic center of the town, is a well-known tourist destination with hotels, villas, and parks. It has a small old town center with narrow streets, shops, and restaurants.

I stayed in one of the many villas just north of Intra, within walking distance of the center of the town. This is where the Italians live and have their summer houses. My villa was close to the lake, the local beach, a sailing club, and a lake restaurant.

Lago Maggiore is 64 km (40 miles) long and 3 to 5 km (2 to 3 miles) wide and covers 212 km^2 (82 square miles). It is Italy's second-largest lake. The northern tip of the lake is inside Switzerland, where the Maggia River (Fiume Maggia) and the Ticino River (Fiume Ticino) enter the lake. After leaving the lake's southern end, the Ticino River is a tributary to the Po River just east of Milan.

Sasso del Ferro

View of Verbania from Sasso del Ferro

You can reach the top of Sasso del Ferro Mountain from Laveno, just across the lake from Verbania. From the ferry port in Laveno, it is just a short walk up to the cable car station, where you will go in either an open or a closed gondola and arrive close to the top of the mountain.

The views from the upper cable car station are superb. To the south, you will see the Po Valley. To the east, you can see Varese town and Lake Varese (Lago di Varese), and to the west, a good view of the southern part of Lago Maggiore. It is a short, relatively steep walk from the cable car station to the top of the mountain.

Experienced hikers can descend by walking back to the lower Cable Car Station, taking the marked routes 222 and 221, 5 km (3 miles) down to Laveno town. The trip will take 2-3 hours.

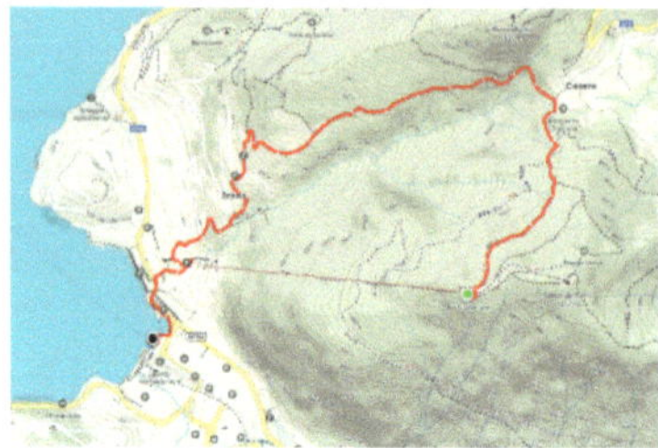

Route 222 & 221to Laveno

Orta San Giulio

Orta San Giulio town at Lago d'Orta

The small town of Orta San Giulio is a half-hour drive southwest of Verbania. With about a thousand inhabitants, it makes for an exciting outing to the most western of the Italian lakes in the foothills of the Alps.

You can take a pleasant walk along the lake shore of the peninsula starting from the parking area just above the northern end of town. Cars are not allowed to enter the town. Piazza Mario Motta is in the town's center on the lake, with many small shops, bars, and restaurants. Opposite the square, you have a view of Isola San Giulio. From the square, there are frequent ferry services to the island. The loop around the peninsula along the lake is slightly more than three kilometers or two miles.

The trip to Orta San Giulio can be combined with a hike in the hills above the town.

Caslano

Caslano town at Lago di Lugano

Caslano is a Swiss town located at the western end of Lake Lugano (Lago di Lugano), close to the Ponte Teresa border town with Italy. You can reach Caslano by car or public transport from Laveno.

The 30-kilometer (20-mile) drive from Laveno will take around three-quarters of an hour. The town center is closed to traffic, but you will find a municipal parking place at Via Chioso and Valle's intersection. On the Piazza Lago, several restaurants have a lake view. A small road and path will take you south of the square around Monte Caslano on a hike of close to 5 km (3 miles).

Chapter Four: Menaggio

Menaggio town in Lago di Como

What makes Menaggio unique?

Menaggio is a relatively short ride from Milan. Still, it is a small, idyllic town with a population of just above 3,000 people. It is located on the western side of Lake Como (Lago di Como) and has a lake promenade with good views of the other lake shores. It is perfect if you want to visit the many exciting places in the area. The main square (Piazza Guiseppe

Garibaldi) is at the southern end of town, close to numerous restaurants and cafes. The car ferry servicing Varenna, located on the eastern side of the lake, originates in Menaggio, where the boats servicing the rest of the lake are also available.

Lago di Como is 46 km (29 miles) long, with a maximum width of 4.5 km (2.8 miles), and covers 146 km2 (56 square miles). It is Italy's third-largest lake. The lake is fed by the Era River (Fiume Era) and the Adda River (Fiume Adda), which enter the lake in the north. After leaving the lake's southern end, the Adda River is a tributary to the Po River.

I picked Menaggio for my visit to Lake Como due to its central location at the lake's western shore, small size, relatively few tourists, and the old town up the hill from the lake with medieval architecture. The town has a well-supplied supermarket, good bus and boat service, and easy access to the mountains and nearby Lago di Lugano. I stayed at a small hotel in the hills just north of the town, which allowed me to take some of the many hikes in the mountains.

Italy's Balcony (Balcone d'Italia)

Balcone d'Italia is located some 35 km (about 22 miles) southwest of Menaggio. On clear days, the balcony offers a spectacular view of Lago di Lugano, Lugano town, and the southern Alps, including Monte Rosa and Matterhorn.

Lago di Lugano and Lugano town

Mount Grona (Monte Grona) Hike

For experienced hikers, one can go to the top of Monte Grona, 1,736 m (5,700 feet) above sea level or around 1,500 m (5,000 feet) above the lake. The trail starts at the parking place in Monti di Breglia, 1,046 m (3432 feet), just 8 km (5 miles) north of Menaggio, and takes you via Rifugio Menaggio to Monte Grona. From Sant Amate, 1,623 m (5324 feet), you follow the lower path to Monti di Breglia. The 7 km (4 miles) hike will take 4-5 hours. The trail is well-marked with red and white signposts, indicating the approximate time between the different points on the hike.

Lago di Como, seen from the hike

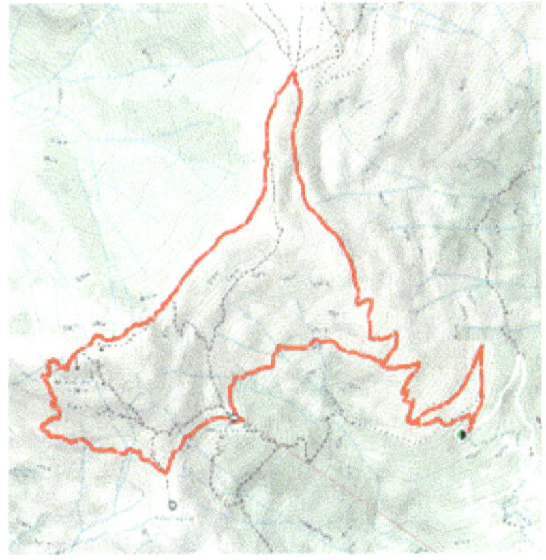

Monte Grona Hike

Lenno to Villa Carlotta Hike

There are several opportunities to walk along Lago di Como around Menaggio. One of the more exciting walks goes between Lenno and Villa Carlotta, just 5 km (3 miles) south of Menaggio. You can begin the hike at Villa Carlotta or, instead, in Lenna, which has more parking opportunities.

Lenno to Villa Carlotta Hike

The 10-kilometer (6-mile) hike will take 3 to 4 hours. The highest point is about 300 m (1,000 feet) above the lake. When you reach Via Belmonte in the small village of Giulino di Mezzegra, you will find a picture of Benito Mussolini and Claretta Petacci on the wall of Villa Belmonte. They were arrested by communist partisans in the village of Dongo north of Menaggio on 27 April 1945 before attempting to escape into Switzerland. They were supposed to be taken to Como at the southern end of the lake the next day and handed over to the Allied forces to stand trial for war crimes. But the next day, they were instead taken to Giulino di Mezzegra by partisans and executed close to Villa Belmonte.

Lago di Como Promenade

When you reach the lake, it is a short walk to the famous Villa Carlotta, one of the many renowned villas in the area. At the end of the hike, you will pass Lenno on the lakeside, where you can find some of the most famous villas on

Lago di Como.

Chapter Five: Sulzano

Sulzano town on Lago d'Iseo

What makes Sulzano unique?

Sulzano is located on the eastern shore of Lake Iseo (Lago d'Iseo), opposite Monte Isola Island. Lago d'Iseo is the fourth largest lake in Lombardy, northeast of Milan, between Lago di Como to the west and Lago di Garda to the east. The lake covers an area of roughly 65 km2 (25 sq miles) and is fed by the Oglio River (Flume Oglio), a tributary to the Po River. A dam at the lake's southwestern end controls the water level at 185 m (607 feet).

Monte Isola and Sulzano town

Sulzano is a small town with a population of around 2,000 people. Its small central square overlooks the lake and is lined with several restaurants. The main ferry line servicing Monte Isola originates in Sulzano, where boats servicing the rest of the lake are also available.

I picked Sulzano for my visit to Lago d'Iseo due to its proximity to Monte Isola, small size, relatively few tourists, and genuine Italian atmosphere. The town has a minor supermarket but is dominated by small, relatively narrow, quiet streets and its Italian population.

Monte Isola

Monte Isola is southern and central Europe's largest lake island, just around 13 square km (5 sq miles). It is believed to have been populated since Roman times. The island obtained special fishing rights in the 15th century and is known for producing fishing nets.

Carzano ferry pier on Monte Isola

Private cars are prohibited, which makes the 9 km (5.5 miles) circular hiking route around the island very pleasant. However, one should be cautious of the scooters used by the local population. The trail passes through several small villages, and several ferries connect the island to the lake shores.

The Ancient Valeriana Route (Antica Strada Valeriana)

Just above Sulzano, you can reach the 24 km (15 miles) long Antica Strada Valeriana route. This route starts at the small village of Pilzone d'Iseo just south of Sulzano and ends at Pisogne town on the eastern side of the lake. The trail is well-marked and was the only route to Valle Camonica at the lake's northern end for thousands of years.

Antica Strada Valeriana map

The route has been reestablished as a hiking trail and follows small country roads, dirt tracks, and paved roads with little traffic. Elevated above the lake shore, it gives you unique views of the lake and the surrounding mountains. Doing the whole route would take you around 6 to 9 hours, but it is also possible to do bits and pieces of the route, which can be combined with rides on the train and the ferry system on the eastern side of the lake. The highest point is just above 900 m (3,000 feet) at the trail's northern end after passing the Zone village in the Orbes Valley (Val Orbes) at roughly 700 m (2,300 feet) above the lake.

Lake view from Antica Strada Valeriana

Camonica Valley (Valle Camonica)

Valle Camonica, formed by Flume Oglio, holds a unique assembly of rock carvings with art and scripture (petroglyphs). The rock carvings are centered around the town of Capo di Ponte. They constitute the largest collections of prehistoric petroglyphs in the world. The National Prehistoric Museum of Valle Camonica (Museo Nazionale della Valle Camonica) is a unique archaeological museum containing some outstanding ancient, decorated rocks and artifacts from the valley. The rock carvings are between 13,000 to 10,000 years old.

Rock carving shows fish, river, and animals

The Camunni people lived in Valle Camonica during the Iron Age (1st millennium BC). The Camunni were among the most significant producers of rock art in Europe. They had a written language, which has been found on around 170 rocks. The alphabet is a variant of the North-Etruscan alphabet, known as the Camunian alphabet.

Chapter Six: Lazise

Lazise town on Lago di Garda's southeastern shore

What makes Lazise unique?

The relatively small town of Lazise on the Eastern side of Lake Garda (Lago di Garda), with around 6,000 people, is well worth a visit during the spring or autumn when there are fewer tourists. Lazise can be reached after a two-hour journey east of Milan. The well-preserved castle and the town walls, with three gates equipped with drawbridges, are from the 14th century. Since the 15th century, the town has been under Venetian, French, and Austrian rule and finally became part of the Kingdom of Italy in 1866.

If you can set aside two days for your visit to Lazise, you will have ample time to walk around the town, go for hikes along the lake to the north and south of the town, and enjoy some of the many bars and restaurants in town. The view of the lake, the setting sun, and the Alps give the town a picturesque setting.

Lazise promenade in center of town

Sirmione

Sirmione town

Sirmione, a town of around 8,000 people, is located some 18 km (11 miles) southwest of Lazise, or about half an hour's drive by car. As with Lazise, visiting the town during spring or autumn is highly recommended when there are fewer tourists. Sirmione has been a resort town for around 2,000 years, beginning with the wealthy families in Verona who used the town for that purpose.

Sirmione can only be visited on foot, but several parking spots are available south of the Sirmione peninsula. A 3 km (2 miles) hike will take you from the parking area to the peninsula's northern end. One of the main attractions on the peninsula is the ancient Grotte di Catullo, the ruins of a large Roman villa built in the 1st century BC.

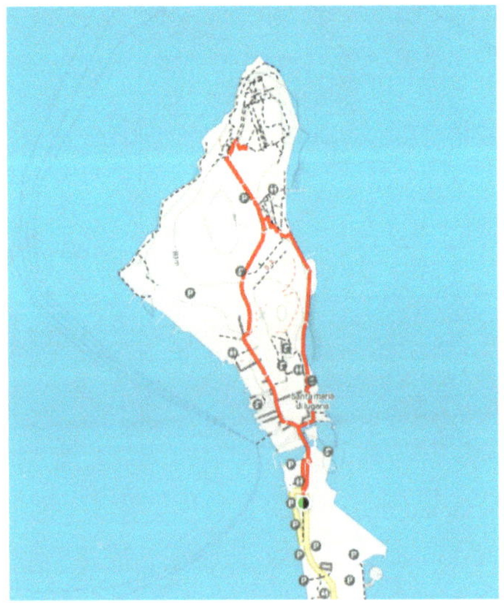

Sirmione Penisula loop

The Scaligero Castle, built in the 13th century at the entrance to the peninsula, was a medieval port fortification, one of Italy's best-preserved castles, and a garrison until the 19th century.

Chapter Seven: Trieste

Trieste town on the Adriatic

What makes Trieste unique?

Even though it is not located on any of the Italian lakes, I highly recommend including Trieste in your visit to northern Italy. Trieste is located at the north end of the Adriatic Sea and has a unique history spanning thousands of years. The city became a Roman colony in 46 BC under Julius Caesar, who named it Tergeste.

In the Middle Ages, Trieste was a maritime rival to Venice, which tried to control the city in the 13th and 14th centuries. In 1381, Trieste became part of the Habsburg Empire.

Trieste town hall

Trieste was part of the Habsburg and Austrian-Hungarian Empires until the end of the 1st World War when Italy annexed it. The city was the empire's only ocean harbor. At the end of the 2nd World War, it came under American and British military administration. The city-state was divided into three zones, and the Allied command administered the northern zone until 1954, when the territory joined Italy. The two southern zones are now part of Slovenia and Croatia.

Today, the city is part of the autonomous region of Friuli-Venezia Giulia and the regional decentralization entity of Trieste. It has a humid subtropical climate and is home to close to 400,000 people in the metro area.

The city's central part features several classic buildings from the time of the previous Austrian Hungarian rule.

Besides walking along the impressive waterfront, visiting the Roman Forum on San Giusto Hill above the city center, next to the San Giusto Castle, is worthwhile. The castle houses a museum with sculptures and antiquity artifacts.

The Miramare Castle

Miramare Castle

The Miramare Castle was built in the second half of the 19th Century. The castle can be reached by bus from the city center or by walking close to four km (2,5 miles) along the promenade in a northerly direction.

Dobrovo (Slovenia)

Dobrovo in southwestern Slovenia

Dobrovo is an hour's drive and around 60 km (37 miles) northwest of Trieste, in Slovenia's Foothills of the Julian Alps. Dobrovo is located in the Littoral region of Slovenia, close to the Italian border, and is the administrative center of the Municipality of Brda. The Municipality of Brda constitutes the Slovenian section of the Gorizia Hills (Goriska Brda in Slovene), which has a Mediterranean climate and is the main wine-producing area in Slovenia. The Dobrovo Castle, located near the town center, was built in the 17th century and houses an art gallery and a museum.

Dobrovo Castle

The area around Dobrovo is dominated by gentle hills covered by many vineyards and olive groves. Numerous well-marked hiking trails can take you through the area, which is often compared with the scenery in parts of Tuscany. A good starting point for the hikes is at the castle in Dobrovo. Wine tasting can be arranged if you call the vineyards beforehand, and Dobrovo has a very well-stocked wine sale shop right in the center of the town.

Dubrovo surroundings

Palmanova (Italy)

Palmanova in western Italy

Palmanova is an hour's drive and around 50 km (30 miles) northwest of Trieste. It is close to the Slovenian border and around 20 km (12 miles) from the Adriatic Sea. The town covers an area of 13 km2 and has a population of around 5,500 people. The construction of Palmanova was inspired by Thomas More's book Utopia, published in 1516. Utopia means a good place in English, but Thomas More later published a supplement to the book and clarified that the title should have been Eutopia, meaning a place of felicity. The book describes an imaginary island in the New World with no private property, with people's needs being stored in warehouses and people requesting what they need. Most people work in agriculture, and women do the same work as men. There was no unemployment, and people only had to work six hours daily. Palmanova was founded by the Venetian Republic in 1593 as a new type of utopian settlement. The first part of the town took 30 years to complete, and the surrounding fortifications were first completed in 1813. When it was first completed in 1622, nobody wanted to live in the town, so the Venetian Republic had to pardon criminals and support them with building materials if they settled there.

Modern Palmanova town plan

The modern town has a pleasant central square, and one can take a relaxing hike on the fortifications north of the town, marked by a black dotted line on the above town plan.

THE ART OF TRAVELLELING
- IN THE FOOTHILLS OF THE SOUTHERN ALPS